In *A Story About Afiya*, my partner James Berry created a magic world for Afiya in which everything she sees and experiences leaves a new picture on her dress, strangely, every day. Anna Cunha has re-imagined the poem and created an enchanting fantasy landscape for Afiya's adventures. This book is a wonderful weaving together of two imaginations.

Myra Barrs

First published in the United Kingdom in 2020 by Lantana Publishing Ltd., London.
www.lantanapublishing.com

American edition published in 2020 by Lantana Publishing Ltd., UK.
info@lantanapublishing.com

Text © James Berry, 1991
Illustration © Anna Cunha, 2020

This poem is reproduced by kind permission of the Estate of James Berry.

The moral rights of the author and illustrator have been asserted.

Distributed in the United States and Canada by Lerner Publishing Group, Inc.
241 First Avenue North, Minneapolis, MN 55401 U.S.A.
For reading levels and more information, look for this title at www.lernerbooks.com
Cataloging-in-Publication Data Available.

Printed and bound in China.
Original artwork using mixed media, finished digitally.

ISBN: 978-1-911373-33-9
ISBN: 978-1-911373-45-2 eBook

A Story About
AFIYA

Afiya: a Swahili name, meaning health,
is pronounced Ah-fee-yah

LANTANA
PUBLISHING

Afiya has fine black skin
that shows off her white clothes
and big brown eyes that laugh
and long limbs that play.

She has a white summer frock
she wears and washes every night
that every day picks on something
to collect, strangely.

Afiya passes sunflowers and finds
the yellow fringed black faces there,
imprinted on her frock, all over.

Another time she passes red roses
and there the clustered bunches
are, imprinted on her frock.

She walks through high grass and sees
butterflies and all kinds
of slender stalks and petals
patterned on her back and front
and are still there, after
she has washed her dress.

Afiya stands. She watches
the sharp pictures in colour,
untouched by her wash.

Yet, next morning, every day,
the dress is cleared and ready,
hanging white as new paper.

Then pigeons fly up before her
and decorate her dress
with their flight and group design.

Afiya goes to the zoo;
she comes back with two tigers
together, on her back and on her front.

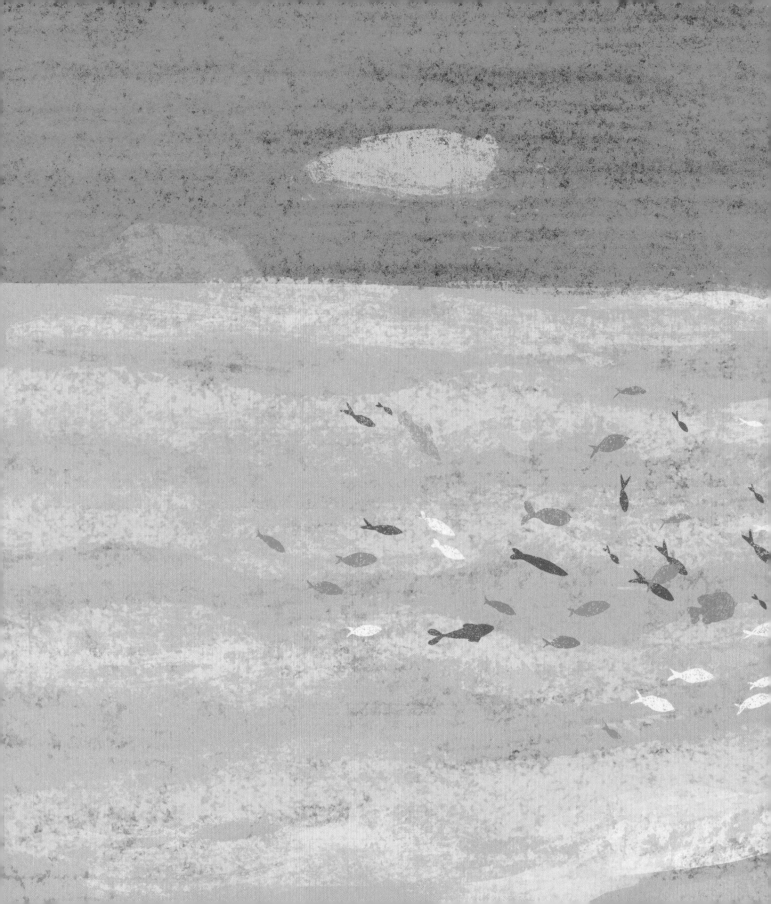

She goes to the seaside;
she comes home with fishes
under ruffled waves
in the whole stretch of sea
imprinted on her dress.

She walks between round and towered
boulders and takes them away,
pictured on her.

Always Afiya is amazed,
just like when she comes home
and finds herself covered
with windswept leaves
of October, falling.